Prayers for Abdulaziz

may Allah forgive him

دعاء في ثواب المغفور له

عبدالعزيز العبدالله

رحمه الله

INTRODUCTION

All praise be to Allah ﷻ the supreme, all-perfect Being who, in His adoration for perfection has bestowed the perfect book, the Qur'an, on the perfect Prophet, Muhammad ﷺ, of the perfect religion.

Allah has allowed the followers of these perfect entities, a beautiful method of asking for favours, from Him. This is the way of du'a.

While we respect the various methods and wordings of ad'iya of the pious, we give preference to the ad'iya that can be found in the Qur'an and Sunnah. These are many in number, thus we present but a few in this publication, and we supplicate that Allah benefits us all from the virtues of them.

THE PROPHETIC SUPPLICATIONS WHEN ENTERING AND LEAVING THE BATHROOM

The Prophet ﷺ has recommended the following:

a. One should not touch the private parts with the right hand when urinating,
b. One should not also use the right hand to clean oneself from excrement.
c. Neither urinate nor defecate with one's front or rear towards the direction of Prayer when outdoor.
d. One should not urinate in flowing water
e. One should not talk with anyone in the bathroom.

Bhukari, Muslim, Abu Dawud and Tirmidhi

1. On the authority of Anas ﷺ, 'The Prophet ﷺ used to say when entering the bathroom :

اَللّٰهُمَّ اِنِّيْ اَعُوْذُبِكَ مِنَ الْخُبُثِ وَالْخَبَآئِثِ

ALLĀHUMMA INNĪ A`ŪDHU BIKA
MINAL KHUBUTHI WAL KHABĀ'ITH

O Allah! I seek refuge in You from demons, male and female.

Bukhari

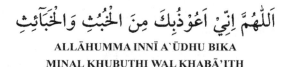

2. On the authority of 'Aishah ﷺ 'The Prophet ﷺ used to say when leaving the bathroom :

غُفْرَانَكَ

GHUFRĀNAK

(O Lord!) I beseech Your forgiveness.

Ahmad and Abu Dawud

THE PROPHETIC MANNERS IN PERFORMING WUDHU (ABLUTION)

The Messenger of Allah ﷺ used to observe the following manners when performing *Wudhu*;

a. To begin *Wudhu* by mentioning the name of Allah ﷻ.
b. To use the *Siwak* (tooth stick) also known as Miswaak.
c. To perform *Wudhu* well (properly).
d. To begin with the right when washing arms and legs.
e. To avoid extravagance in using water.
f. To wet between the fingers and toes.
g. To wet his beard.
h. To let water reach as much of the mouth and nostrils as possible, unless fasting, when one should do so sparingly.
i. To say on completion of *Wudhu*.

اَشْهَدُ اَنْ لَّا اِلٰهَ اِلَّا اللهُ وَحْدَهُ لَا شَرِيْكَ لَهُ

وَاَشْهَدُ اَنَّ مُحَمَّدًا عَبْدُهُ وَرَسُوْلُهُ

ASH-HADU 'ALLĀ ILĀHA ILLAL-LĀHU WAḤDAHŪ
LĀ SHARĪKA LAH. WA ASH-HADU ANNA
MUḤAMMADAN `ABDUHŪ WA RASŪLUH

***I testify that there is no god but Allah,
the One, who has no partner and
I testify that Muhammad is His servant and Messenger.*** (3)

رَبِّ اغْفِرْلِيْ ذَنْبِيْ وَوَسِّعْ لِيْ فِيْ دَارِيْ
وَبَارِكْ لِيْ فِيْ رِزْقِيْ

**RABBIGH-FIRLĪ DHAMBĪ WA WASSI`
LĪ FĪ DĀRĪ WA BĀRIKLĪ FĪ RIZQĪ**

***O Lord! forgive me my sins, make my house spacious
and bless for me my provision.*** (4)

j. To perform two Rakah (other than the obligatory ones) after Wudhu. (5)

1. *Ibn Majah reported on the authority of Abi Sa'id ﷺ that the Prophet ﷺ said, "No ablution is valid for one who does not mention the Name of Allah at the beginning of it."*
2. *The various sunnan are narrated in many books including Al-Bukhari, Muslim, Imam Ahmad and Ibn Majah.*
3. *Abu Dawud in his Sunan.*
4. *Muslim reported of 'Uqbah Ibn 'Amir Ibn Al-Khattab ﷺ that the Messenger of Allah ﷺ said, "Whoever performs ablution perfectly, then says, 'I testify that there is no god but You and Muhammad is the servant of Allah and His Messenger, will have the eight gates of Paradise open for him so that he can choose which one to enter from."*
5. *Ibn As-Sunni*

THE PROPHET'S SUPPLICATION WHEN OVERWHELMED BY A PROBLEM

Ja'far Ibn Muhammad related from his father who related from his father that when the Messenger of Allah ﷺ was overwhelmed by any trouble he used to say:

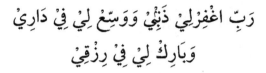

اَللّٰهُمَّ احْرُسْنِيْ بِعَيْنِكَ الَّتِيْ لَا تَنَامُ وَاكْنُفْنِيْ بِكَنَفِكَ الَّذِيْ
لَا يُرَامُ وَارْحَمْنِيْ بِقُدْرَتِكَ عَلَيَّ فَلَا اَهْلِكُ وَاَنْتَ
رَجَآئِيْ فَكَمْ مِّنْ نِّعْمَةٍ اَنْعَمْتَ بِهَا عَلَيَّ قَلَّ لَكَ بِهَا
شُكْرِيْ وَكَمْ مِّنْ بَلِيَّةٍ اِبْتَلَيْتَنِيْ بِهَا قَلَّ لَكَ بِهَا صَبْرِيْ
فَيَا مَنْ قَلَّ عِنْدَ نِعْمَتِهٖ شُكْرِيْ فَلَمْ يَحْرِمْنِيْ
وَيَا مَنْ قَلَّ عِنْدَ بَلِيَّتِهٖ صَبْرِيْ فَلَمْ يَخْذُلْنِيْ
وَيَا مَنْ رَّاٰنِيْ عَلَى الْخَطَايَا فَلَمْ يَفْضَحْنِيْ
يَا ذَا الْمَعْرُوْفِ الَّذِىْ لَا يَنْقُضُ أَبَدًا وَّيَا
ذَا النِّعْمَةِ الَّتِيْ لَا تُحْصٰى عَدَدًا اَسْأَلُكَ اَنْ تُصَلِّيَ
عَلٰى مُحَمَّدٍ وَّعَلٰى اٰلِ مُحَمَّدٍ وَّبِكَ اَدْرَأُ فِيْ نُحُوْرِ
الْأَعْدَآءِ وَالْجَابِرِيْنَ اَللّٰهُمَّ اَعِنِّيْ عَلٰى دِيْنِيْ بِالدُّنْيَا
وَعَلٰى اٰخِرَتِيْ بِالتَّقْوٰى وَاحْفَظْنِيْ فِيْمَا غِبْتُ عَنْهُ
وَلَا تَكِلْنِيْ اِلٰى نَفْسِيْ فِيْمَا حَضَرْتَهٗ عَلَيَّ يَا مَنْ

لَّاتَضُرُّهُ الذُّنُوْبُ وَلَا يُنْقِصُهُ الْعَفْوُ هَبْ لِيْ مَا لَا
يُنْقِصُكَ وَاغْفِرْلِيْ مَا لَا يَضُرُّكَ اِنَّكَ اَنْتَ الْوَهَّابُ اَسْأَلُكَ
فَرَجًا قَرِيْبًا وَّصَبْرًا جَمِيْلًا وَّرِزْقًا وَّاسِعًا وَّالْعَافِيَةَ
مِنَ الْبَلَايَا وَشُكْرَ الْعَافِيَةِ

ALLĀHUM-MAḤRUSNĪ BI`AYNIKAL-LATĪ LĀ
TANĀMU WAKNUFNĪ BI KANAFIKAL-LADHĪ LA
YARĀMU WARḤAMNĪ BI QUDRATIKA `ALAYYA
FALĀ AHLIKU WA ANTA RAJĀ'Ī FAKAM-MIN
NI`MATIN AN`AMTA BIHĀ `ALAYYA
QALLA LAKA BIHĀ SHUKRĪ.
WA KAM MIM BALIYYATI-NIBTALAYTANĪ
BIHĀ QALLA LAKA BIHĀ ṢABRĪ.
FA YĀ MAN QALLA `INDA
NI`MATIHĪ SHUKRĪ FA LAM YUḤRIMNĪ.
WA YĀ MAN QALLA `INDA BALIYYATIHĪ
ṢABRĪ FA LAM YAKHDHILNĪ.
WA YĀ MAR-RA'ĀNĪ `ALAL KHAṬĀYĀ FA LAM YUFḌIḤNĪ.
YĀ DHAL MA`RŪFIL-LADHĪ LĀ YANQUḌU ABADĀ.
WA YĀ DHAN NI`MATIL-LADHĪ LĀ TUḤṢĀ `ADADĀ.
AS'ALUKA AN TUṢALLIYA `ALĀ
MUḤAMMADIW-WA `ALĀ ĀLI MUḤAMMAD.
WA BIKA ADRA'U FĪ NUḤŪRIL-A`DĀ'I WAL JĀBIRĪN.
ALLĀHUMMA A`INNĪ `ALĀ DĪNĪ BIDDUNYĀ
WA `ALĀ ĀKHIRATĪ BIT-TAQWĀ WAḤFAẒNĪ

FĪMĀ GHIBTU `ANH.
WALĀ TAKILNĪ ILĀ NAFSĪ FĪMĀ ḤAḌARTAHŪ `ALAYY.
YĀ MAL-LĀ TAḌURRUHUDH-DHUNŪBU WA LĀ
YUNQIṢUHUL `AFWU HAB LĪ MĀ LĀ
YUNQISUKA WAGHFIRLĪ MĀ LĀ YAḌURRUK.
INNAKA ANTAL WAHHĀB.
AS'ALUKA FARAJAN QARĪBAW WA ṢABRAN
JAMĪLAW WA RIZQAW WĀSI`AW WAL`ĀFIYATA
MINAL BALĀYĀ WA SHUKRAL `ĀFIYAH.

O Allah! keep watch over me with Your sleepless Eye.
Protect me with Your Protection.
Forgive me with Your Power so that I will never
perish because You are my hope.
O Allah! my gratitude ever falls short from thanking
Your bounties and my patience ever fails
when You put me on trials.
O You have not deprived me (of Your bounties)
when seeing my shortcomings, Who has not
severed me when seeing my impatience,
Who have not uncovered me when seeing my faults.
O Ever Gracious, the One Whose bounties cannot be numbered!
I ask You to bless Muhammad and his household
and I beseech You against all the tyrannical enemies.
O Allah! Assist me concerning my religion by
means of my world and assist me concerning my
next World by means of piety.
O Allah! save me from that which I have no
knowledge of and do not leave me alone with
myself in what I have knowledge of.
O You Who are neither harmed by sins
nor limited by pardon!
Pardon me for You are the Most Gracious

and grant me speedy relief, good patience,
abundant provision and gratitude to safety.

Musnad Al-Firdaws

In another narration:

اَسْأَلُكَ الشُّكْرَ عَلَى الْعَافِيَةِ اَسْأَلُكَ الْغِنٰى عَنِ النَّاسِ
وَلَا حَوْلَ وَلَا قُوَّةَ اِلَّا بِاللهِ الْعَظِيْمِ

AS'ALUKASH-SHUKRA `ALAL `ĀFIYAH.
AS'ALUKAL GHINĀ `ANIN-NĀSI WA LĀ ḤAWLA
WA LĀ QUWWATA ILLĀ BILLĀHIL `AẒĪM.

O Allah! Make me grateful for granting me wellbeing
and I ask You to make me independent of needing people.
There is no might or power but with Allah,
the Exalted and the Glorious.

On the authority of Abu Hurairah ﵁ who said that the Prophet ﷺ said, "I have never been overwhelmed by a problem but Jibril appeared to me (in any form) saying, 'O Muhammad say:

تَوَكَّلْتُ عَلَى الْحَيِّ الَّذِيْ لَا يَمُوْتُ وَالْحَمْدُ لِلّٰهِ الَّذِيْ
لَمْ يَتَّخِذْ وَلَدًا وَّلَمْ يَكُنْ لَّهٗ شَرِيْكٌ فِي الْمُلْكِ وَلَمْ
يَكُنْ لَّهٗ وَلِيٌّ مِّنَ الذُّلِّ وَكَبِّرْهُ تَكْبِيْرًا

TAWAKKALTU `ALAL ḤAYYIL-LADHĪ LĀ YAMŪTU

WAL ḤAMDU LILLĀHIL-LADHĪ LAM
YATTAKHIDH WALADAW-WA LAM YAKUL-LAHŪ
SHARĪKUN FIL MULKI WA LAM YAKUL
LAHŪ WALIYYUM MINADH-DHULLI
WA KABBIRHU TAKBĪRĀ.

I place my trust on the Living One Who does not die.
Praise be to Allah Who begets no son,
and has no partner in (His) dominion:
nor does He need to protect Himself from humiliation.
(So) magnify Him for His greatness and glory."'

At Tabarani.

SUPPLICATIONS FOR PRAISING ALLAH THE ALMIGHTY

سُبْحَانَ اللهِ وَبِحَمْدِهِ لَا قُوَّةَ اِلَّا بِاللهِ مَا شَآءَ اللهُ كَانَ
وَمَا لَمْ يَشَأْ لَمْ يَكُنْ اَعْلَمُ اَنَّ اللهَ عَلٰى كُلِّ شَيْءٍ قَدِيْرٌ
وَاَنَّ اللهَ قَدْ اَحَاطَ بِكُلِّ شَيْءٍ عِلْمًا

SUBḤĀNAL-LĀHI WA BI ḤAMDIHĪ LĀ
QUWWATA ILLĀ BILLĀHI MĀ SHĀ'AL-LĀHU
KĀNA WA MĀ LAM YASHA' LAM YAKUN.
A`LAMU ANNAL-LĀHA `ALĀ KULLI SHAY'IN QADĪR.
WA ANNAL-LĀHA QAD AḤĀṬA BI KULLI SHAY'IN `ILMĀ.

Glory be to Allah and with His Praise.
There is no power save in Allah.
What Allah wills, will be,
and what He does not will, will not.

*I know that Allah has power over all things and
that He comprehends all things in (His) Knowledge.*

سُبْحَانَ اللهِ وَبِحَمْدِهٖ عَدَدَ خَلْقِهٖ وَرِضَا
نَفْسِهٖ وَزِنَةَ عَرْشِهٖ وَمِدَادَ كَلِمَاتِهٖ

**SUBḤĀNAL-LĀHĪ WA BI ḤAMDIHĪ `ADADA
KHALQIHĪ WA RIḌĀ NAFSIHĪ WAZINATA `ARSHIHĪ
WA MIDĀDA KALIMĀTIH.**

*Glory be to Allah and praise be to Him,
in the expanse of His creation, as much as He pleases,
as much as the weight of His Throne,
and as much as the ink it would take
to record all His Words.*

سُبْحَانَ رَبِّيَ الْعَلِيِّ الْأَعْلَى الْوَهَّاب

SUBḤĀNA RABBIYAIL `ALIYYIL A`LAL WAHHĀB

*Glory be to my Lord, the Ever-exalted,
the Most High and the Bestower.*

اَللّٰهُمَّ لَكَ الْحَمْدُ كَمَا يَنْبَغِي لِجَلَالِ
وَجْهِكَ وَعَظِيْمِ سُلْطَانِكَ

**ALLĀHUMMA LAKAL ḤAMDU KAMĀ YAMBAGHĪ
LIJALĀLI WAJ-HIKA WA`AŻĪMI SULṬĀNIK.**

O Allah! to You is praise as appropriate to the Majesty of Your Face and the Magnificence of Your Sovereignty.

اَللّٰهُمَّ لَكَ الْحَمْدُ كُلُّهُ وَلَكَ الْمُلْكُ كُلُّهُ وَبِيَدِكَ الْخَيْرُ
كُلُّهُ وَاِلَيْكَ يَرْجِعُ الْاَمْرُ كُلُّهُ عَلاَنِيَتُهُ وَسِرُّهُ
فَاَهْلاً اَنْتَ اَنْ تُحْمَدَ اِنَّكَ عَلٰى كُلِّ شَيْءٍ قَدِيْرٌ

ALLĀHUMMA LAKAL ḤAMDU KULLUHŪ WALAKAL MULKU KULLUHŪ WABI YADIKAL KHAYRU KULLUHŪ WA ILAYKA YARJI`UL AMRU KULLUHŪ `ALĀNIYATUHŪ WA SIRRUH. FA 'AHLAN ANTA AN TUḤMAD. INNAKA `ALĀ KULLI SHAY'IN QADĪR.

O Allah! All praise is due to You.
Yours is all sovereignty.
All good is in Your Hands.
To You is (the determination of) all affairs,
both the hidden and the manifest.
You are the most deserving to be praised
and You have power over all things.

اَللّٰهُمَّ لَكَ الْحَمْدُ كُلُّهُ
لَا قَابِضَ لِمَا بَسَطْتَّ وَلَا بَاسِطَ لِمَا قَبَضْتَ
وَلَا هَادِيَ لِمَنْ اَضْلَلْتَ وَلَا مُضِلَّ لِمَنْ هَدَيْتَ

وَلَا مُعْطِيَ لِمَا مَنَعْتَ وَلَا مَانِعَ لِمَا اَعْطَيْتَ
وَلَا مُقَرِّبَ لِمَا بَاعَدْتَ وَلَا مُبَاعِدَ لِمَا قَرَّبْتَ

ALLĀHUMMA LAKAL ḤAMDU KULLUH LĀ QĀBIḌA LIMĀ BASAṬTA WA LĀ BĀSIṬA LIMĀ QABAḌTA WA LĀ HĀDIYA LIMAN AḌLALTA WA LĀ MUḌILLA LIMAN HADAYT.
WA LĀ MU`ṬIYA LIMĀ MANA`TA WA LĀ MĀNI`A LIMĀ A`ṬAYT.
WA LĀ MUQARRIBA LIMĀ BĀ`ADTA WA LĀ MUBĀ`IDA LIMĀ QARRABT.

O Allah! Yours is all praise.
There is no one to withhold what You extend,
and no one to extend what You withhold!
There is no one to guide what You lead astray,
and no one to lead astray whom You guide!
There is no one to give what You forbid,
and no one to forbid what You give!
There is no one to bring near what You hold far
and no one to hold far what You bring near.

اَللّٰهُمَّ اَنْتَ اَحَقُّ مَنْ ذُكِرَ وَاَحَقُّ مَنْ عُبِدَ وَاَنْصَرُ
مَنِ ابْتُغِيَ وَاَرْأَفُ مَنْ مَّلَكَ وَاَجْوَدُ مَنْ سُئِلَ وَاَوْسَعُ
مَنْ اَعْطٰى اَنْتَ الْمَلِكُ لَا شَرِيْكَ لَكَ وَالْفَرْدُ الَّذِيْ
لَا نِدَّ لَكَ كُلُّ شَيْءٍ هَالِكٌ اِلَّا وَجْهَكَ لَنْ تُطَاعَ

اِلَّا بِاِذْنِكَ وَلَنْ تُعْصٰى اِلَّا بِعِلْمِكَ تُطَاعُ فَتَشْكُرُ

وَتُعْصٰى فَتَغْفِرُ اَقْرَبُ شَهِيْدٌ وَاَدْنٰى حَفِيْظٌ حِلْتَ دُوْنَ

النُّفُوْسِ وَاَخَذْتَ بِالنَّوَاصِي وَكَتَبْتَ الْاٰثَارَ وَنَسَخْتَ

الْاٰجَالَ اَلْقَلْبُ لَكَ مُفْضِيَةٌ وَالسِّرُّ عِنْدَكَ عَلَانِيَةٌ

اَلْحَلَالُ مَا اَحْلَلْتَ وَالْحَرَامُ مَا حَرَّمْتَ وَالدِّيْنُ مَا شَرَعْتَ

وَالْخَلْقُ خَلْقُكَ وَالْعَبْدُ عَبْدُكَ وَاَنْتَ اللهُ الرَّؤُفُ الرَّحِيْمُ

اَسْأَلُكَ بِنُوْرِ وَجْهِكَ الَّذِيْ اَشْرَقَتْ لَهُ السَّمَاوَاتُ

وَالْاَرْضُ وَبِكُلِّ حَقٍّ هُوَ لَكَ وَبِحَقِّ السَّائِلِيْنَ

عَلَيْكَ اَنْ تُقْبِلَنِيْ فِيْ هٰذِهِ الْغَدَاوةِ وَاَنْ تُجِيْرَنِيْ مِنَ النَّارِ

ALLĀHUMMA ANTA AḤAQQU MAN DHUKIR.

WA AḤAQQU MAN `UBID.

WA ANṢARU MANI-BTUGHIYA.

WA AR'AFU MAM-MALAK.

WA AJWADU MAN SU'IL.

WA AWSA`U MAN A`ṬĀ.

ANTAL MALIKU LĀ SHARĪKA LAK.

WAL FARDUL-LADHĪ LĀ NIDDA LAK.

KULLU SHAY'IN HĀLIKUN ILLĀ WAJHAK.

LAN TUṬĀ`A ILLĀ BI'IDHNIK.
WA LAN TU`ṢĀ ILLĀ BI`ILMIK.
TUṬĀ`U FATASHKURU WA TU`ṢĀ FATAGHFIR.
AQRABU SHAHĪDUN WA ADNĀ ḤAFĪẒ.
ḤILTA DŪNAN-NUFŪSI
WA AKHADHTA BIN-NAWĀṢĪ
WA KATABTAL-ĀTHĀRI WA NASAKHTAL-ĀJĀL.
ALQALBU LAKA MUFḌIYAH.
WAS-SIRRU `INDAKA `ALĀNIYAH.
ALḤALĀLU MĀ AḤLALTA
WAL ḤARĀMU MĀ ḤARRAMTA.
WAD-DĪNU MĀ SHARA`TA.
WAL KHALQU KHALQUK. WAL `ABDU `ABDUK.
WA ANTAL-LĀHUR RA'ŪFUR RAḤĪM.
AS'ALUKA BI NŪRI WAJHIKAL-LADHĪ
ASHRAQAT LAHUS-SAMĀWĀTI WAL ARḌU
WA BI KULLI ḤAQQIN HUWA LAK,
WA BI ḤAQQIS-SĀ'ILĪN `ALAYKA AN TUQAB-BĪLANĪ
FĪ HĀDHIHIL-GHADĀTI WA AN TUJĪRANĪ MINAN-NĀR.

O Allah! You are the Most deserving to be remembered,
the Most deserving to be worshiped,
the Most victorious among those who are sought,
the Most clement among those who are owned,
the Most generous among those who are asked,
the Most bounteous among those who give.
You are the Sovereign, there is no partner besides You.
You are the One, to You there is no peer.
Everything will perish save You Face.
You will never be obeyed save by Your permission,
and will never be disobeyed save by Your permission.
Being obeyed, You thank, being disobeyed You forgive.

You are the most near Witnessing (One)
and the most near Preserver.
You came in between the souls,
seized the foreheads,
wrote (all things) people left behind,
and recorded periods (for everything).
Before You, all hidden secrets of the hearts are revealed.
The lawful is what You permit,
the unlawful is what You prohibit,
and the Religion is what You legislated.
Creation is Yours and the servant is Yours and
You are the Ever Compassionate, the Ever Merciful.
I ask You with the Light of Your Face to which
the heavens and the earth are shining,
with every right which is Yours,
and with the right of those who ask You
to accept me in this morning and
to protect me against the Fire.

اَلْحَمْدُ لِلّٰهِ الَّذِيْ لَمْ يَتَّخِذْ وَلَدًا وَّلَمْ يَكُنْ لَّهٗ شَرِيْكٌ
فِي الْمُلْكِ وَلَمْ يَكُنْ لَّهٗ وَلِيٌّ مِّنَ الذُّلِّ وَكَبِّرْهُ تَكْبِيْرًا

ALḤAMDU LILLĀHIL-LADHĪ LAM YATTAKHIDH
WALADAW-WA LAM YAKUL-LAHŪ SHARĪKUN
FIL MULKI WA LAM YAKUL LAHŪ WALIYYUM
MINADH-DHULLI WA KABBIRHU TAKBĪRĀ.

Praise be to Allah, Who begets no son,
and has no partner in (His) dominion:
nor (needs) He any to protect Him from humiliation:
Yea, magnify Him for His Greatness and Glory.

اَللّٰهُ اَكْبَرُ اَللّٰهُ اَكْبَرُ اَللّٰهُ اَكْبَرُ وَلِلّٰهِ الْحَمْدُ
سُبْحَانَ اللّٰهِ وَالْحَمْدُ لِلّٰهِ وَلَا اِلٰهَ اِلَّا اللّٰهُ وَاللّٰهُ اَكْبَرُ
وَلَا حَوْلَ وَلَا قُوَّةَ اِلَّا بِاللّٰهِ الْعَلِيِّ الْعَظِيْمِ

ALLĀHU AKBAR. ALLĀHU AKBAR.
ALLĀHU AKBAR. WA LILLĀHIL ḤAMD.
SUBḤANAL-LĀHI WAL ḤAMDU LILLĀHI WA LĀ
ILĀHA ILLAL-LĀHU WALLĀHU AKBAR.
WA LĀ ḤAWLA WA LĀ QUWWATA ILLĀ
BILLĀHIL `ALIYYIL `AẒĪM.

Allah is the Greatest, Allah is the Greatest,
Allah is the Greatest. All praise be to Allah...
Glory be to Allah, praise be to Allah,
there is no god but Allah,
Allah is the greatest, and there is no power
nor strength save in Allah,
the Most High, the Magnificent.

اَللّٰهُ اَكْبَرُ كَبِيْرًا وَّالْحَمْدُ لِلّٰهِ كَثِيْرًا
وَّسُبْحَانَ اللّٰهِ بُكْرَةً وَّاَصِيْلًا

ALLĀHU AKBAR KABĪRĀ.
WALḤAMDU LILLĀHI KATHĪRĀ.
WA SUBḤĀNAL-LĀHI BUKRATAW WA AṢĪLĀ

Surely Allah is the Greatest.

His is the abundant praise.
Glory to Him day and night.

اَللّٰهُ اَكْبَرُ اَللّٰهُ اَكْبَرُ اَللّٰهُ اَكْبَرُ مِمَّا نَخَافُ وَنَحْذَرُ

ALLĀHU AKBAR. ALLĀHU AKBAR.
ALLĀHU AKBARU MIMMĀ NAKHĀFU WA NAḤDHAR.

Allah is the Greatest, Allah is the Greatest,
Allah is the Greatest from what we fear or watch over.

اَللّٰهُ اَكْبَرُ اَللّٰهُ اَكْبَرُ اَللّٰهُ اَكْبَرُ عَدَدَ ذُنُوْبِنَا حَتّٰى تُغْفَرَ

ALLĀHU AKBAR. ALLĀHU AKBAR. ALLĀHU AKBARU
`ADADA DHUNŪBINĀ ḤATTĀ TUGHFAR.

Allah is the Greatest, Allah is the Greatest,
Allah is the Greatest equal to the number of
our sins until they are forgiven.

SUPPLICATION OF QUNUT

اَللّٰهُمَّ اِنَّا نَسْتَعِيْنُكَ وَنَسْتَغْفِرُكَ وَنُؤْمِنُ بِكَ وَنَتَوَكَّلُ
عَلَيْكَ وَنُثْنِيْ عَلَيْكَ الْخَيْرَ وَنَشْكُرُكَ وَلَانَكْفُرُكَ وَنَخْلَعُ
وَنَتْرُكُ مَنْ يَّفْجُرُكَ ۝ اَللّٰهُمَّ اِيَّاكَ نَعْبُدُ وَلَكَ نُصَلِّيْ
وَنَسْجُدُ وَاِلَيْكَ نَسْعٰى وَنَحْفِدُ وَنَرْجُوْ رَحْمَتَكَ وَنَخْشٰى

عَذَابَكَ اِنَّ عَذَابَكَ بِالْكُفَّارِ مُلْحِقٌ ط

ALLĀHUMMA INNĀ NASTA`ĪNUKA WANASTAGH-FIRUKA WA NU'MINU BIKA WANATAWAK-KALU `ALAYKA WANUTHNĪ `ALAYKAL KHAYR WANASH-KURUKA WALĀ NAKFURUKA WANAKHLA`U WANATRUKU MAY-YAFJURUK. ALLĀHUMMA IYYĀKA NA`BUDU WALAKA NUṢALLĪ WANASJUDU WA'ILAYKA NAS`Ā WANAḤFIDU WANARJŪ RAḤMATAKA WANAKHSHĀ ADHĀBAK INNA ADHĀBAKA BILKUFFARI MULḤIQ.

O Allah, we seek Thy help; and ask Thy forgiveness;
and believe in Thee and trust in Thee;
and we praise Thee in the best manner and we thank Thee;
and we are not ungrateful and we cast off
and forsake him who disobeys Thee.
O Allah, Thee alone do we worship, and to Thee we pray;
and before Thee do we prostrate,
To Thee do we turn in haste; and hope for Thy mercy,
and we fear Thy punishment.
Thy punishment surely overtakes the unbelievers.
are at enmity with.
O our Lord! Who are above all things,
Sacred and Exalted!

اَللّٰهُمَّ اهْدِنَا فِيْ مَنْ هَدَيْتَ وَعَافِنَا فِيْ مَنْ عَافَيْتَ
وَتَوَلَّنَا فِيْ مَنْ تَوَلَّيْتَ وَبَارِكْ لَنَا فِيْمَا اَعْطَيْتَ

وَقِنَا بِرَحْمَتِكَ وَاصْرِفْ عَنَّا شَرَّ مَا قَضَيْتَ
إِنَّكَ تَقْضِيْ وَلَا يُقْضٰى عَلَيْكَ إِنَّهٗ لَا يُذِلُّ مَنْ وَّالَيْتَ
وَلَا يُعِزُّ مَنْ عَادَيْتَ تَبَارَكْتَ رَبَّنَا وَتَعَالَيْتَ

ALLĀHUM-MAHDINĀ FĪ MAN HADAYT.
WA `ĀFINĀ FĪ MAN `ĀFAYT.
WA TAWALLANĀ FĪ MAN TAWALLAYT.
WA BĀRIK LANĀ FĪMĀ A`ṬAYT.
WA QINĀ BI RAḤMATIKA WAṢRIF `ANNĀ
SHARRA MĀ QAḌAYT. INNAKA TAQḌĪ
WA LĀ YUQḌĀ `ALAYK.
INNAHŪ LĀ YADHILLU MAW-WĀLAYT.
WA LĀ YA`IZZU MAN `ĀDAYT. TABĀRAKTA
RABBANĀ WA TA`ĀLAYT.

O Allah! Guide us among those You guide,
grant us health and pardon among those
You grant health and pardon,
look after us among all the others whom You look after,
grant us grace in what You have given us,
and protect us from the evil of what You have ordained;
for You decree and none can decree against You,
and none is abased whom You have befriended and
none is exalted whom You

اَللّٰهُمَّ اقْسِمْ لَنَا مِنْ خَشْيَتِكَ مَا تَحُوْلُ بِهٖ بَيْنَنَا وَبَيْنَ
مَعَاصِيْكَ وَمِنْ طَاعَتِكَ مَا تُبَلِّغُنَا بِهٖ جَنَّتَكَ

وَمِنَ الْيَقِيْنِ مَا تُهَوِّنُ بِهِ عَلَيْنَا مَصَآئِبَ الدُّنْيَا وَمَتِّعْنَا
بِأَسْمَاعِنَا وَاَبْصَارِنَا وَقُوَّتِنَا مَا اَبْقَيْتَنَا وَاجْعَلْهُ الْوَارِثَ
مِنَّا وَاجْعَلْ ثَأْرَنَا عَلٰى مَنْ ظَلَمَنَا وَانْصُرْنَا عَلٰى مَنْ
عَادَانَا وَلَا تَجْعَلْ مُصِيْبَتَنَا فِيْ دِيْنِنَا وَاجْعَلِ الْجَنَّةَ
هِيَ دَارَنَا وَلَا تُسَلِّطْ عَلَيْنَا مَنْ لَّا يَخَافُكَ فِيْنَا
وَلَا يَرْحَمُنَا بِرَحْمَتِكَ يَآ اَرْحَمَ الرَّاحِمِيْنَ

ALLĀHUM-MAQSIMLANĀ MIN KHASHYATIKA
MĀ TAḤŪLU BIHĪ BAYNANĀ WA BAYNA MA`ĀṢIK.
WA MIN ṬĀ`ATIKA MĀ TUBALLIGHUNĀ BIHĪ JANNATAK.
WA MINAL YAQĪNI MĀ TUHAWWINU BIHĪ `ALAYNĀ
MAṢĀ'IBAD DUNYĀ. WA MATTI`NĀ BI ASMĀ`INĀ WA ABṢĀRINĀ
WA QUWWATINĀ MĀ ABQAYTANĀ.
WAJ`ALHUL WĀRITHA MINNĀ.
WAJ`AL THA'RANĀ `ALĀ MAN ŻALAMANĀ.
WANṢURNĀ `ALĀ MAN `ĀDANĀ.
WA LĀ TAJ`ĀL MUṢĪBATANĀ FĪ DĪNINĀ.
WAJ`ALIL JANNATA HIYA DĀRANĀ.
WA LĀ TUSALLIṬ `ALAYNĀ MAL-LĀ YAKHĀFUKA
WA LĀ YARḤAMUNĀ.
BI RAḤMATIKA YĀ ARḤAMAR RĀḤIMĪN.

O Allah! Distribute between us the heedfulness

necessary to come between us and the commission of wrong against You; and the obedience necessary to gain for us admission to Your Paradise, and the unswerving faith necessary to minimize for us the tribulations of this world. O Allah! Allow us to enjoy our hearing, our sight and our strength for as long as we live, and make that enjoyment our heir (so that when we are gone those who have benefitted through us will remember to pray for us), and place our vengeance on those who have wronged us, and give us victory over our enemies, and try us not in our faith, make Paradise our abode, give not power over us to those who would not fear You, and would oppress us, O the most merciful of those who show mercy!

اَللّٰهُمَّ اِنَّكَ عَفُوٌّ تُحِبُّ الْعَفْوَ فَاعْفُ عَنَّا

ALLĀHUMMA INNAKA `AFUWWUN
TUḤIBBUL `AFWA FA`FU `ANNĀ.

O Allah! You are Ever-Forgiving and loves forgiveness, so forgive us.

اَللّٰهُمَّ لَا تَدَعْ لَنَا فِيْ مَقَامِنَا هٰذَا ذَنْبًا اِلَّا غَفَرْتَهٗ
وَلَا هَمًّا اِلَّا فَرَّجْتَهٗ وَلَا دَيْنًا اِلَّا قَضَيْتَهٗ وَلَا مَرِيْضًا
اِلَّا شَفَيْتَهٗ وَلَا مُبْتَلٰى اِلَّا عَافَيْتَهٗ وَلَا مَيِّتًا اِلَّا رَحِمْتَهٗ

وَلَا عَدُوًّا اِلَّا خَذَلْتَهُ وَلَا حَاجَةً مِّنْ حَوَآئِجِ الدُّنْيَا
وَالْاٰخِرَةِ هِيَ لَكَ رِضًا وَّلَنَا فِيْهَا صَلَاحٌ اِلَّآ اَعَنْتَنَا
قَضَآئِهَا وَيَسَّرْتَهَا بِرَحْمَتِكَ يَا اَرْحَمَ الرَّاحِمِيْنَ

ALLĀHUMMA LĀ TADA` LANĀ FĪ MAQĀMINĀ
HĀDHĀ DHAMBAN ILLĀ GHAFARTAH.
WA LĀ HAMMAN ILLĀ FARRAJTAH.
WA LĀ DAYNAN ILLĀ QAḌAYTAH.
WA LĀ MARĪḌAN ILLĀ SHAFAYTAH.
WA LĀ MUBTALĀ ILLĀ `ĀFAYTAH.
WA LĀ MAYYITAN ILLĀ RAḤIMTAH.
WA LĀ `ADUWWAN ILLĀ KHADHILTAH.
WA LĀ ḤĀJATAM MIN ḤAWĀ'IJID-DUNYĀ WAL
ĀKHIRATI HIYA LAKA RIḌAW WA LANĀ FĪHĀ ṢALĀḤUN ILLĀ
A`ANTANĀ QAḌĀ'AHĀ WA YASSARTAHĀ.
BI RAḤMATIKA YĀ ARḤAMAR RĀḤIMĪN.

O Allah! Leave no sins of ours in this
assembly without being forgiven.
Nor any grief without being relieved,
nor any debt without it being paid,
nor any sick without it being healed,
nor any affliction without it being recovered,
nor any misguidance without guidance,
nor any transgression without it being ceased,
nor anyone has died without their sins being forgiven,
nor any enemies without being humiliated,
nor any difficulty without it being facilitated,

Printed in Great Britain
by Amazon

23533930R00020